COLOR
YOURSELF HAPPY
POSTCARDS
50 POSITIVE PASSAGES
TO COLOR
AND SHARE

M0000075930

Thunder Bay Press
An imprint of Printers Row Publishing Group
THUNDER BAY   10350 Barnes Canyon Road, Suite 100, San Diego, CA 92121
P·R·E·S·S   www.thunderbaybooks.com

Published in the French language originally under the title:
50 messages – pensées positives à colorier et à envoyer
© 2014, Editions First, an imprint of Edi8, 12 avenue d'Italie, 75013 Paris, France

Printers Row Publishing Group is a division of Readerlink Distribution Services, LLC.
The Thunder Bay Press name and logo are trademarks of Readerlink Distribution Services, LLC.

All notations of errors or omissions should be addressed to Thunder Bay Press, Editorial Department, at the above address.
All other correspondence (author inquiries, permissions) concerning the content of this book should be addressed to Édition First,
an imprint of Édi8, Paris, France

Thunder Bay Press
Publisher: Peter Norton
Publishing Team: Lori Asbury, Ana Parker, Laura Vignale
Editorial Team: JoAnn Padgett, Melinda Allman, Dan Mansfield

ISBN: 978-1-62686-664-5

Printed in China

20 19 18 17 16 2 3 4 5 6

At the end you will find blank cards for creating your own drawings and positive messages!

COLOR YOURSELF HAPPY POSTCARDS

50 POSITIVE PASSAGES TO COLOR AND SHARE

LISA MAGANO AND CHARLOTTE LEGRIS

THUNDER BAY
P · R · E · S · S
San Diego, California

Every day is a new beginning.

Today's defeat is tomorrow's victory.

ADDITIONAL
POSTAGE
REQUIRED

ADDITIONAL
POSTAGE
REQUIRED

The healer holds the healing.

Rain is the promise of sun.

ADDITIONAL
POSTAGE
REQUIRED

Eating,
DRINKING,
sleeping,
LOVING,
laughing—
THE FIVE PILLARS
OF LIFE.

The path is the destination. Enjoy the journey.

Your daily life is a treasure.
Guard it carefully.

ADDITIONAL
POSTAGE
REQUIRED

Live each day like an entire lifetime.

Every problem is a chance to grow.

ADDITIONAL
POSTAGE
REQUIRED

Life is short, so savor your time.

We succeed when it's our deepest desire.

ADDITIONAL
POSTAGE
REQUIRED

ADDITIONAL
POSTAGE
REQUIRED

Simplicity is the greatest wealth.

ADDITIONAL
POSTAGE
REQUIRED

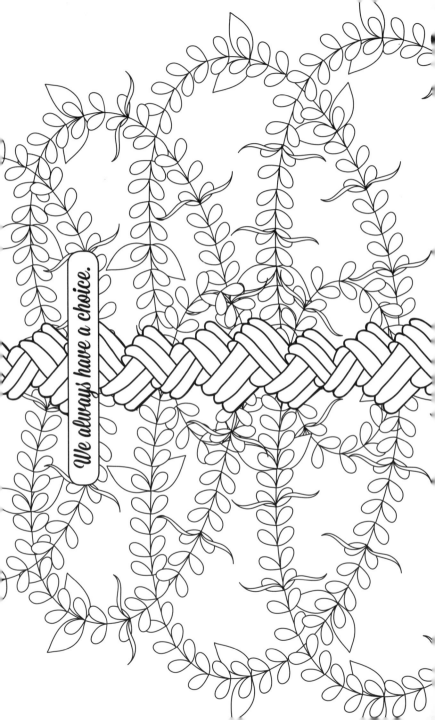

We always have a choice.

Happiness is doing it

ADDITIONAL
POSTAGE
REQUIRED

My destiny is my life's work.

ADDITIONAL
POSTAGE
REQUIRED

GIVE UP *OF* OBSTACLES IN THE FACE

AND *you* *don't* *have* to *give* up

your FREEDOM.

ADDITIONAL
POSTAGE
REQUIRED

To feel is to be alive.

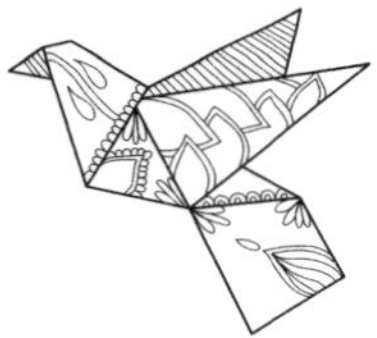

ADDITIONAL
POSTAGE
REQUIRED

ADDITIONAL
POSTAGE
REQUIRED

The truth will always prevail.

ADDITIONAL
POSTAGE
REQUIRED

Be rather than have.

ADDITIONAL
POSTAGE
REQUIRED

Live for today, hope for tomorrow.

TODAY
I WILL CHOOSE
JOY.

Small steps can take you far.

Humor is the key to open all doors.

ADDITIONAL
POSTAGE
REQUIRED

Turn anger into energy.

ADDITIONAL
POSTAGE
REQUIRED

Some things are not important. Move on.

ADDITIONAL
POSTAGE
REQUIRED

Stop waiting for the storm to end – admire the lightning.

ADDITIONAL
POSTAGE
REQUIRED

YOU NEED TALENT TO SUCCEED—BUT MOSTLY COURAGE.

ADDITIONAL
POSTAGE
REQUIRED

Time is a gift.

Make peace with yourself.

Imagination
is an inalienable right.

I breathe, therefore I am

I am, therefore I breathe

Luck is the skill
to spot
opportunities.

ADDITIONAL
POSTAGE
REQUIRED

Do what you love to love what you do.

prefer joy to hope.

ADDITIONAL
POSTAGE
REQUIRED

The ideal is in our imperfection.

ADDITIONAL
POSTAGE
REQUIRED

ADDITIONAL
POSTAGE
REQUIRED

Meditation is a date with yourself.

Kindness forges the strongest bonds.

ADDITIONAL
POSTAGE
REQUIRED

When you laugh every day, you're taking good care of yourself.

ADDITIONAL
POSTAGE
REQUIRED

*Nothing is possible without thinking,
and thinking makes everything possible.*